Timeline of castle history

9th-10th centuries

Timber castles appear in northwestern France.

Later 12th century

Circular and polygonal keeps are built for the first time.

1179-1214

English kings Henry II and John build Dover Castle, the first in Europe to have a double ring of defensive walls.

1051

First castles in England recorded.

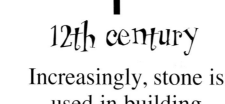

12th century

Increasingly, stone is used in building castles.

Late 10th century

Earliest known stone keeps appear in the Loire Valley, France.

1190s

Richard I of England adds a large extra bailey (courtyard surrounded by a defensive wall) to the Tower of London.

15th century

Castles become less important in military strategy as conflicts are increasingly settled on the battlefield rather than by sieges.

1238

Henry III extends the Tower of London's defensive walls northward and eastward, doubling the castle's area.

18th century

Castle ruins are considered 'picturesque'.

13th century

Concentric walls, rather than the keep, become the castle's strongest line of defence. Firearms appear for the first time in the West.

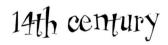

16th century

Increasingly, lords prefer to build themselves comfortable houses rather than castles.

14th century

Castle design reaches its fullest development in northern Europe.

Map of castles across Britain and Europe

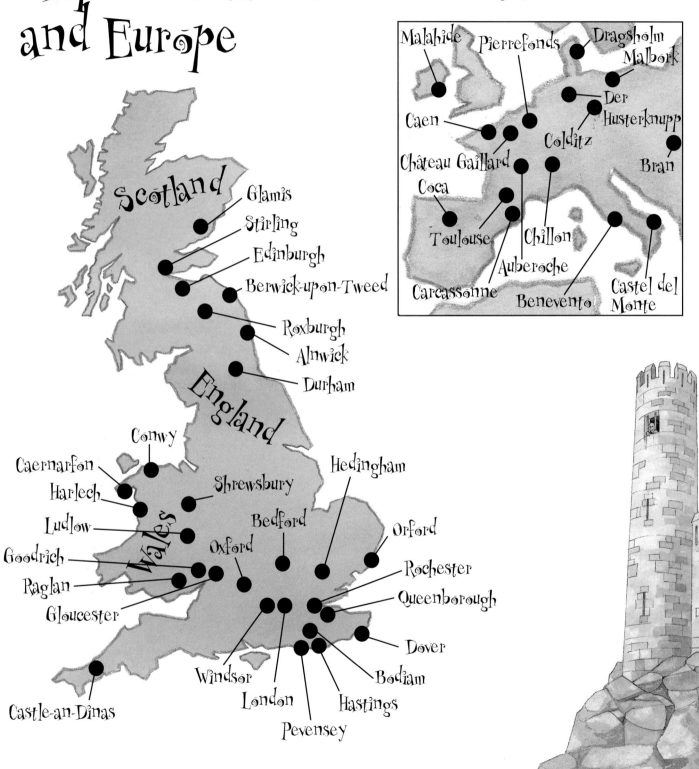

Scotland

Glamis

Stirling

Edinburgh

Berwick-upon-Tweed

Roxburgh

Alnwick

Durham

England

Conwy

Caernarfon

Harlech

Ludlow

Goodrich

Raglan

Gloucester

Wales

Shrewsbury

Oxford

Bedford

Hedingham

Orford

Rochester

Queenborough

Dover

Bodiam

Windsor

London

Pevensey

Hastings

Castle-an-Dinas

Malahide

Pierrefonds

Dragsholm

Malbork

Caen

Der Husterknupp

Colditz

Château Gaillard

Bran

Coca

Toulouse

Chillon

Auberoche

Carcassonne

Benevento

Castel del Monte

Author:
Fiona Macdonald studied history at
Cambridge University and at the University of
East Anglia. She has taught in schools, adult
education and university and is the author of
numerous books for children on historical topics.

Artist:
David Antram was born in Brighton, England,
in 1958. He studied at Eastbourne College of Art
and then worked in advertising for fifteen years
before becoming a full-time artist. He has
illustrated many children's non-fiction books.

Series creator:
David Salariya was born in Dundee,
Scotland. He has illustrated a wide range of books
and has created and designed many new series for
publishers both in the UK and overseas. In 1989,
he established The Salariya Book Company. He
lives in Brighton with his wife, illustrator Shirley
Willis, and their son Jonathan.

Editor:
Karen Barker Smith

Published in Great Britain in MMXIV by
Book House, an imprint of
The Salariya Book Company Ltd
25 Marlborough Place, Brighton BN1 1UB
www.salariya.com
www.book-house.co.uk

PB ISBN-13: 978-1-909645-57-8

S A L A R I Y A

© The Salariya Book Company Ltd MMXIV

1 3 5 7 9 8 6 4 2

A CIP catalogue record for this book is available
from the British Library.

Printed and bound in Singapore.

Visit our website at www.book-house.co.uk
or go to www.salariya.com for **free** electronic versions of:
You Wouldn't Want to be an Egyptian Mummy!
You Wouldn't Want to be a Roman Gladiator!
You Wouldn't Want to be a Polar Explorer!
You Wouldn't Want to sail on a 19th-Century Whaling Ship!

PAPER FROM
SUSTAINABLE
FORESTS

You Wouldn't Want to Be in a Medieval Dungeon!

Criminals, traitors and outlaws better watch out!

Written by
Fiona Macdonald

Illustrated by
David Antram

Created and designed by
David Salariya

Prisoners You'd Rather Not Meet

BOOK HOUSE
a SALARIYA *imprint*

Contents

Introduction 5

A career change 6

Who will you work for? 8

Types of prisons 10

Castle life 12

Criminals, traitors and outlaws 14

Bad company 16

Innocent victims 18

Dealing with prisoners 20

Rats, lice and fleas 22

The soft option 24

No escape! 26

Freedom or death 28

Glossary 30

Index 32

Introduction

It is the end of the 15th century in medieval England. You are a tough, battle-scarred soldier who has just returned home after fighting wars in faraway countries. You are happy to have survived, even though your shoulder has been badly wounded and your arm is broken.

You won't be much use as a fighter from now on, but your injuries are healing and you start to feel better. You're also feeling poor! You have spent all your soldier's wages and have nothing to live on. You need to find a job so you decide to go to the nearest castle, to see what work is available there. You're in luck! The castle needs someone to help run its prison and the captain of the guard asks if you would like the job. Think carefully! Do you really want to work in a medieval gaol?

A career change

If you become a castle gaoler you will have to work hard and learn quickly. The job is not well paid, but you have power over your prisoners. You will find many ways of making extra money, by demanding bribes and charging fees. There is a good chance of promotion. Experienced prison warders and 'turnkeys' (security guards) are in demand – most castles, cities and towns have at least one gaol. All this means that there are plenty of other people who would like the job.

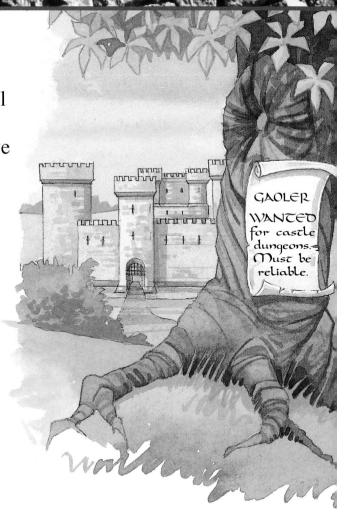

GAOLER WANTED for castle dungeons. Must be reliable.

Applicants for the job:

AN OLD SERVANT. He knows the castle well and has worked here since he was a boy.

A CRUSADER. Back home after fighting wars in the Middle East, he needs a new job.

A PRIEST. Clever and cunning, he's on the lookout for people who break Church laws.

A MONK. He's in charge of the punishment cell at the local monastery.

A NIGHT-WATCHMAN. He guards the castle gates and is looking for promotion.

I'd steer clear of that place if I were you. Some of those prisoners are a nasty lot!

Handy hint

Women need not apply! Only men can be gaolers in the Middle Ages.

AN IRON-WORKER. He's made all the metal bars that stop prisoners escaping.

THE LOCAL CONSTABLE. He works for the sheriff and arrests people who break the law.

A LOCAL TOWNSMAN. He hopes to make money from working at the gaol.

A TRUSTED OFFICIAL. Elegant and polite, he would be good at dealing with captive nobles and royalty.

A THUG. He will frighten the prisoners but they'll probably outwit him.

7

Who will you work for?

L ike all medieval gaolers, you will not have special training. If you get the job it will be because the person who owns the prison thinks you can be trusted. It is most likely that your employer will be the king. It's his duty to maintain law and order and to protect his kingdom from traitors, rebels and foreign enemies. Most prisons in London belong to him, plus the shire (county) gaols and dungeons in all the royal castles. But many other powerful people have their own private prisons too.

Possible employers

Lady   *Lord*   *Commander*

LORDS AND LADIES rule the land around their castles and have their own private prisons. They can punish minor crimes, such as trespass, slander and non-payment of rent.

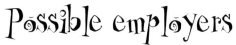
Bishop

BISHOPS can imprison people who break the Church's religious laws. The bishops often get involved in quarrels over Church land and property.

ABBOTS AND ABBESSES are in charge of religious communities. If monks and nuns break the rules, they are locked in a punishment cell.

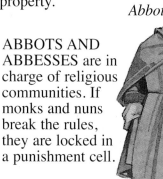
Abbot

Religious investigator
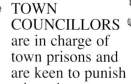

ARMY COMMANDERS imprison enemy captives and demand a ransom to set them free.

TOWN COUNCILLORS are in charge of town prisons and are keen to punish crimes by merchants, such as fraud and theft.

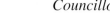
Councillor

RELIGIOUS INVESTIGATORS. Their mission is to get rid of heresy (unlawful beliefs) by torturing confessions out of suspects.

SHERIFFS act as the king's deputy in each shire. Criminals are held in a royal prison until the king's judges hold a trial.

Sheriff

IN MEDIEVAL ENGLAND the king's word is law! The most important royal court is called the 'King's Bench'. It gets its name from the seat used by top royal judges, who try suspects accused of serious crimes. Sometimes the king himself sits in the court. Other judges normally visit gaols once or twice a year. They hear the evidence against prisoners accused of less serious crimes and decide whether they are innocent or guilty.

9

Types of prisons

Once you start work, you will soon discover that prisons are not all the same. In castles, prison cells are often built above the main gates in the outer walls. This way, dangerous prisoners cannot get too close to the castle keep. Other castle prisons are hidden deep below ground or in high towers. Sometimes cells are just metal cages hung outside the castle. King Edward I of England kept the wife of a Scottish noble in a cage like this for over a year! City prisons are often built in draughty vaults below the chambers where councillors meet. Empty buildings are sometimes turned into prisons. In Southwark, south of London, the busiest prison is a converted inn called the White Swan.

AN OUBLIETTE (left) is a narrow, tube-shaped prison, without windows. The only way in is through a trapdoor at the top. Prisoners are lowered down on a rope and left to rot! Sometimes water seeps in from the bottom and they drown.

Oubliette

YOU MIGHT have to shut prisoners in a 'little ease' – a tiny room, hollowed out of castle walls (right). Some of these cramped chambers are so small that prisoners cannot lie down, sit comfortably or even turn around.

Bottle dungeon

Handy hint

Once you have gained experience, give advice to builders and architects. They might pay you for tips on how to make a prison really secure.

Bottle dungeons (left) are deep underground prisons. Tall stone towers (right) keep prisoners high in the air. Both are designed to prevent escapes and hide prisoners away from friends who might help them.

What have I done to deserve this?

SOME CASTLES have private rooms where rich or noble prisoners are locked up in nice surroundings. They may even be allowed to stroll in the castle's gardens (above).

Little ease

11

Castle life

Life in a medieval castle is extremely busy. It is like a whole village community inside strong stone walls. There is never a quiet moment, from sunrise to after dark. There are soldiers shouting, blacksmiths hammering, horses whinnying, pigs grunting, babies crying, women chattering, workmen grumbling, messengers cursing and, above it all, the lord of the castle barking out commands. Heavy farm carts, full of vital supplies, rumble over the stone courtyard. Labourers grunt and sweat as they unload sacks of grain. It's no wonder you can't sleep in your off-duty hours!

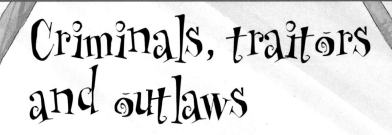

Criminals, traitors and outlaws

As a gaoler, you'll have to deal with people accused of many different crimes. There are highway robbers, counter-feiters, traitors and other 'enemies of the state'. All will have been arrested on suspicion and put in prison to wait for months or years for judges to arrive. Take care! Many prisoners will be angry, violent or despairing and some of them are dangerous. All will be frightened that one day soon, they might die. Death is the punishment for serious crimes such as murder, treason, forgery or robbery with violence.

Dead scared

All these prisoners (right) face the death penalty if they are found guilty. People who commit less serious crimes are fined, flogged or left to rot in prison for a while.

Pirate   *Murderer*   *Burglar*

Traitor or rebel   Plotter   Outlaw   Counterfeiter   Corrupt official

Bad company

You will probably believe that most of your prisoners are a bad lot, even though many of them have not committed a crime. Some are in prison because they have powerful enemies. People are also imprisoned because they are thought to be witches or have strange beliefs. Some prisoners will be there simply through bad luck. Other prisoners are certainly guilty, but hardship and poverty might have forced them into stealing or breaking the law. However, like most medieval people, you think that people should accept their fate and have no excuse to break the law.

SHEEP STEALING. A nice fat sheep makes a tempting target for hungry thieves. It can feed a poor family for at least a week.

STOP, THIEF!

LIFE IS HORRIBLE for ordinary people in the Middle Ages. Most are poor and many are not free to leave their lord's lands. They are often cold, tired and hungry. It is not surprising that some become criminals.

THE CATHOLIC CHURCH is powerful throughout Europe. Church leaders believe that only they know the truth about God. Anyone with different beliefs is guilty of heresy, which is a deadly sin.

Handy hint

See what advice you can get from any 'witches' in your prison. Such people often know about healing herbs, poisons and 'magic spells'.

HOME LIFE can be stressful. Many people have arranged marriages. Whatever their feelings, husbands and wives have to stay together, or starve. There is no state welfare system so poverty drives people to commit crime.

SOLDIERS CAPTURED IN BATTLE face a gloomy future. They will be kept in prison until their families pay a ransom to set them free. If they cannot afford to do this, then the soldiers may be killed.

17

Innocent victims

I t is hard to dislike all your prisoners – some are innocent victims with heartbreaking stories. Often these people have found themselves behind bars because somebody powerful wants them out of the way. Maybe they have angered the royal family or know embarrassing secrets. Perhaps they have rival claims to inherit a rich estate or even the throne! Many such prisoners are women and children. The young English princes, Edward, aged 12, and Richard, aged 9 (right), were locked in the Tower of London by their uncle, King Richard III, in 1483. He then had them murdered so they could not grow up and take over his throne.

SHIPWRECKED SAILORS are arrested and locked up until they can prove who they are.

FRIENDS who have quarrelled with someone powerful may be carried off to gaol.

WOMEN WHO REJECT royal offers of love or marriage might be put in prison until they change their minds.

FOREIGN AMBASSADORS are sent to prison when wars begin. They were friends before, but have suddenly become enemies.

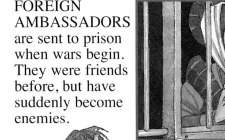

ROYAL WIVES who fail to give birth to a son might be shut away because they are useless!

PEOPLE WITH MENTAL ILLNESSES are locked up, to keep them safe, but others cruelly come to laugh at them.

Handy hint

Invite the public to visit your prison. They'll pay you to let them gawp at pretty princesses, wounded warriors or people who are mentally ill.

Wh...what was that noise?

Dealing with prisoners

Medieval prisons are terrible places. Most prisoners will beg you to set them free or at least move them out of the damp, dark, crowded cells. You must be hardhearted. If you let anyone escape, you'll lose your job, be beaten, or even executed!

I'll give you anything you want if I get out of here, just for a piece of that pie!

CONDITIONS INSIDE gaols are disgusting. But most gaolers do not care! If prisoners cannot arrange for someone to bring them food, candles and bedding they will suffer terribly.

Cells are slimy...

damp...

dark...

and crowded!

20

Prisoners will plead for food, water and other basic comforts, such as straw to sleep on or the chance to warm themselves by a fire in winter. Nothing – no food, water or bedding – is supplied by the owner of the gaol. Prisoners' friends and families must provide these items. You can offer to get supplies, if the prisoners can pay you!

YOU CAN MAKE extra money by demanding a fee from the friends, business colleagues and lawyers who visit prisoners (left).

YOU MIGHT LET starving prisoners beg for food through the bars of their cells (right). With luck, passers-by will take pity on them.

No beds

No toilets

21

Rats, lice and fleas

You need a strong stomach and a strong mind to cope with prison conditions. Most cells are infested with insects and most prisoners are covered with lice or hopping with fleas. Rats, lizards, beetles and cockroaches scurry across the damp, dirty floors. As well as scaring sensitive prisoners, these creatures can carry serious diseases. The worst are typhus fever and plague, also known as the Black Death! Many prisoners die from disease before they ever come to trial. Prisons are also very smelly. Inside, they reek of stale blood, sweat and sewage. Outside most prison walls, you can't escape the smell of stagnant moats, blocked drains, privies and stables.

I'm dying to get out of here...

RAIN, SNOW and cold, damp air blow through the prison bars and chill everyone locked up inside. Many prisoners die from hypothermia (extremely low body temperature).

FLEAS carry plague germs in their saliva. Lice carry the germs that cause typhus fever. If the bugs bite you, you will catch these diseases.

RATS also carry plague, a terrible illness. Victims get huge boils in their groins and armpits, bleed from the mouth (and elsewhere), run a high temperature, become delirious and die.

DIRTY, SMELLY WATER carries germs and tiny microorganisms that cause vomiting and diarrhoea. Prisoners have to risk drinking it – or die of thirst.

Handy hint

Copy the judges who hold trials in prisons. They carry posies of herbs and flowers because they believe the sweet smell will kill diseases carried in foul air.

The soft option

Sometimes it's a good idea to treat prisoners kindly, especially those who might be in a position to help you if they're set free. Even the most powerful men and women will be grateful if you make their stay in prison as comfortable as possible. Let them bring their own books, furniture, musical instruments, servants and children. Let them continue to have a hobby or work. Top tailors imprisoned in London bring their sewing kits with them so that they can still make clothes for customers. This way they earn money to pay for luxuries while behind bars.

EVEN THE MOST COMFORTABLE PRISONS can be dangerous places. Poison or 'accidents' are the most usual methods of quietly getting rid of important prisoners. The Duke of Clarence was found drowned in a cask of wine at the Tower of London, in 1478!

Is there anything I can do for you, m'lady?

EXERCISE stops prisoners growing restless and dangerous. The guards at Fleet prison, in London, let rich prisoners play skittles all day long.

WIVES AND MOTHERS often ask to bring food in for their families. Let them do this, but search the meals for hidden weapons or tools.

FRIARS need your permission to preach and say prayers in prison. Welcome them! Their holy words might help your sinful soul.

What a creep!

Handy hint

There will be some visitors your prisoners don't want to see, such as enemies who could taunt or bully them. Offer to keep them out – for a fee!

LOOK FORWARD to a better job! You may get this as a reward from powerful people you have helped in gaol.

YOU CAN EXPECT gifts and bribes in return for treating prisoners kindly. Don't be too greedy!

BE POLITE to important people, even if they are prisoners. They might be powerful again one day.

No escape!

There are plenty of ways to ensure your prisoners are secure. To begin with, you'll rely on heavy wooden doors with strong locks and bolts, and iron bars across all the windows. You will probably choose to keep the most dangerous or high-risk prisoners fastened to cell walls, using handcuffs and leg-fetters that are attached to heavy iron chains. If you are cruel, you can arrange for these to be fixed so the prisoner can't move or can't touch the floor.

To force prisoners to confess to crimes gaolers use torture. The most common tortures are: the red-hot iron, which burns; the rack, which stretches prisoners and destroys their joints; the boot, which crushes prisoners' legs; and thumbscrews, which squeeze fingers until the fingernails fall off.

Leg-fetters

No! Not the red-hot iron!

This might sting just a little bit...

Handy hint

Fancy new locks are being invented all the time. Don't be too keen to use them! You might lock yourself in — and no one would know how to set you free!

Pillory

Stocks

Ducking stool

Other punishments

THIEVES can be locked in a pillory (above left) where their heads and hands are trapped while the public throws rubbish at them. Or you could shut them in the stocks (above right) so that everyone they've cheated on can pelt them with mud and rotten food.

IF A WOMAN is known to be a gossip and scold, then tie her to a ducking stool (left) and dip her in the river. That will teach her to hold her tongue!

27

Freedom or death

Very few prisoners manage to escape from gaol or can pay the vast sums of ransom money to be set free. Those with powerful friends can expect to be released if a new king comes to the throne or when new politicians win power. Most prisoners find that death is the only way out of gaol. They die in prison from cold, hunger, torture or disease – or they are executed. Noble men and women are beheaded, which is quick and almost painless. Ordinary criminals are condemned to be hanged – a slow, very painful way to die.

Can't we talk about this...?

Not guilty

SOME PRISONERS get out of gaol more peacefully. They might be found not guilty and set free. They might be forgiven their crimes and receive a royal pardon. They might escape in disguise. Or they might die and be free from suffering at last.

Handy hint

Retire as soon as you can! As a gaoler, you'll have made many enemies. Some people will look for revenge – you don't want to end up in gaol yourself!

Death

Escape in disguise

A pardon

SAVED BY A SONG! King Richard the Lionheart of England (ruled 1189–1199) was captured by enemies while returning from a war. No one knew where he was being held. Legend tells that his minstrel travelled Europe, singing Richard's favourite song while looking for him. When the king sang back, the minstrel knew he had found him!

29

Glossary

Abbess The leader of a religious community of nuns.

Abbot The leader of a religious community of monks.

Ambassador A senior government official sent to represent his or her king and country overseas.

Bottle dungeon A deep underground prison, shaped like an old-fashioned bottle. Prisoners entered through a narrow 'bottle neck' and were kept captive in the globe-shaped chamber below.

Bribe A payment made in return for a special favour.

Counterfeiter A person that makes fake coins.

Crusader A Christian soldier who fought against Muslim armies in the Middle East.

Fetters Curved iron bars that could be locked around prisoners' legs.

Flogged Severely beaten.

Fraud Cheating.

Friar A priest who lived close to poor and needy people in medieval communities.

Gaol Another word for prison; sometimes spelt 'jail'.

Heresy Unlawful religious beliefs. In the Middle Ages that included any beliefs that were different from those of the people in power.

Keep The strong central tower of a castle.

Medieval Belonging to the Middle Ages (the years from around AD 1000 to AD 1500).

Middle Ages (see **Medieval** above).

Minstrel A medieval travelling musician who played an instrument and performed songs and poetry.

Outlaw A criminal who lives outside the normal rules of law.

Pardon To excuse or forgive someone for a wrongdoing and release them from punishment.

Plague A deadly and infectious disease which was very widespread in the Middle Ages.

Ransom A demand for money in order to let prisoners go free.

Scold The medieval word for a woman who was always telling off other people or gossiping.

Slander Telling lies about someone.

Stocks A low wooden frame with holes for a criminal's feet. Offenders were locked in the stocks as a punishment.

Tenant A person who rents land and property from the person who owns it.

Traitor A person who betrays their country. In the Middle Ages, people who betrayed their local lord or their employer might be accused of being traitors. A wife who betrayed her husband could also be considered a traitor.

Trespass To enter someone's private property without permission.

Vaults Cellars or underground rooms.

Index

A
abbots and abbesses 8

B
bishops 8
bottle dungeons 11
bribes 6, 9, 21, 24, 25

C
captive enemies 8, 17, 18
castles 5, 6, 8, 10, 11, 12, 13
Church laws 8, 16
constables 7
criminals 9, 14, 15, 16, 17, 28
Crusaders 6

D
death penalty 14, 15, 20, 28, 29
dirt and disease 20, 21, 22, 23, 28
dungeon (*see* prison)

E
escape 11, 20, 26, 28, 29

F
fines 14
flogging 14
food and water 20, 21, 23, 24

G
gaol (*see* prison)
guards 5, 6, 13

H
heresy 8, 16

I
innocent victims 18, 19
iron-workers 7, 12

J
judges 8, 9

K
kings 8, 9, 18, 28, 29

L
law and order 8, 9, 14, 15
little ease 10, 11
living conditions 16, 17
locks and chains 26, 27

M
mental illness 18, 19
monks 6, 8

N
nobles 7, 8, 10, 11, 12, 18, 24, 25, 28

O
oubliette 10
outlaws 14, 15

P
pardon 29
pillory 27
poison 24
priests 6, 18, 24
prisoners 6, 7, 14, 15, 16, 17, 18, 19, 20, 21, 22, 23, 24, 25, 26, 27, 28, 29
prisons 5, 6, 8, 10, 11, 14, 20, 21, 22, 23, 24, 25, 26, 28
  conditions 20, 21, 22. 23, 24, 25, 26
  design 10, 11, 26, 27
promotion 6, 25

R
ransom 28
rats 21, 22, 23
retirement 29

S
sheriffs 8

smells 22, 23
soldiers 5, 12, 17, 19
stocks 27

T
torture 25, 26, 28
towers 10, 11
town councillors 8
training 8
traitors 8, 14, 15

V
visitors 19, 25

W
witches 16, 17
women 6, 10, 11, 12, 15, 17, 18, 19, 24, 27, 28

Some grisly castle siege deaths

At the siege of Antioch, Turkey (1097–1098), a Turk killed by Godfrey of Bouillon was riding so fast he was sliced in half 'like a young leek'. His upper half fell to the ground and his lower half rode on into the city.

In 1417, at Caen, France, a knight called Sir Edward Springhouse fell off a scaling ladder into the ditch below. The French dropped burning straw on him and roasted him in his armour.

Simon de Montfort (French father of the English baron Simon de Montfort) was killed at the siege of Toulouse, France, in 1218 by a mangonel* powered by 'women, ladies, and young girls'. They hit him with a stone that cracked his head open.

At Acre (in present-day Israel), during the Crusades, a knight squatting down to relieve himself was attacked from behind with a lance. ('How base', said the person reporting it, 'to take a knight thus unawares'.) The knight managed to jump aside, grab a stone, fatally bash his attacker on the head with it, and capture his horse.

A machine for hurling missiles

Did you know?

The medieval terms for carving meat are:
- **break** a deer
- **rear** a goose
- **sauce** a capon
- **spoil** a hen
- **unbrace** a mallard
- **display** a crane
- **disfigure** a peacock
- **allay** a pheasant
- **wing** a partridge
- **thigh** a pigeon.

Top spooky castles

Glamis Castle in Scotland is supposedly haunted by the sounds of a furious fight that the first lord of Glamis had with the devil. He was a gambling man with a quick temper. Having no one to play cards with one night, he said he'd sooner play with the devil than with no one. The devil turned up to play. The lord kept losing to him and ranted and raved so loudly that a servant knocked to see if all was well. While the lord went to the door, the devil disappeared, taking, it is said, the lord's soul with him.

Dragsholm Castle in Denmark is said to be the haunt of the ghost of James, Earl of Bothwell, third husband of Mary, Queen of Scots. When Scotland got too dangerous for him after the murder of Mary's second husband, Darnley, he went to Scandinavia. The king of Denmark slapped him in prison at Dragsholm on suspicion of the murder. The pillar he was chained to is still there. Around it is a circular groove, worn into the floor by the earl's feet during the ten years he spent there until he died.

Castle-an-Dinas in Cornwall supposedly has ghosts of soldiers. Ghosts, of course, are only as reliable as the people who see them. An old man interviewed by antiquarian H. Jenner in 1867 reported seeing the ghosts of King Arthur's soldiers practising their drills there. He particularly remembered 'the glancing of the moonbeams on their muskets'. (Think about it!)*

* Muskets had not yet been invented during King Arthur's time.

Malahide, the oldest inhabited castle in Ireland, boasts five ghosts. The best of the bunch are:

- Sir Walter Hussey, from the 15th century, who supposedly wanders about groaning and pointing to a spear wound that killed him in battle (on his wedding day!). His bride then married a rival, and he still can't get over it.

- Miles Corbett, who held the castle after the English Civil War. He signed King Charles I's death warrant and was hung, drawn and quartered for it later. His ghost is said to roam Malahide as a figure in armour that falls into four pieces before your eyes.

The Tower of London is packed with too many famous ghosts to mention. One who is not so famous appeared to a sentry on guard outside the Jewel House in 1816. The guard saw a ghostly bear advancing toward him. It literally frightened him to death, for he reportedly died a few days later.

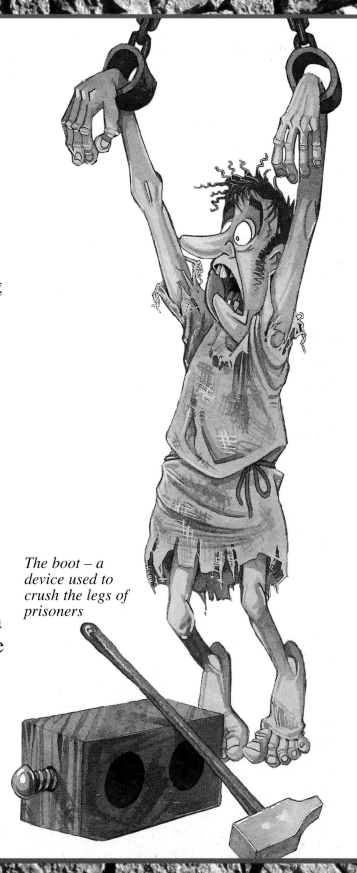

The boot – a device used to crush the legs of prisoners